A New True Book

THE CHUMASH

By Jill D. Duvall

CHILDRENS PRESS®

CHICAGO

Chumash speaker, photographed in 1935

PHOTO CREDITS

The Bettmann Archive–41 (right)

© Reinhard Brucker–30 (bottom); Milwaukee Public Museum, 34

© Ernestine De Soto McGovern–2

Photri–© Arnold J. Kaplan, 9

Courtesy of Anthropological Archives, Smithsonian Institution–© John P. Harrington, 6, 8 (2 photos)

Santa Barbara Museum of Natural History–© Cover, 18, 24 (2 photos), 26, 39; © John P. Harrington, 5 (left), 6; © "Acorns for Supper" artist Jan Timbrook, 14; © "A. Roll of the Dice" artist Jan Timbrook, 30 (top); © "Interior Chumash Village" artist Mlke Ward, 17; © "Antap Dancers at the Siliytk" artist Mike Ward, 28; © Peter Howorth, 22 (large photo); © Rick Terry, 25; © "The Chumash Cosmos: The 3 Worlds" artist Richard Applegate, 33; © Ivan Hunter, 36; © Leon deCessac, 37 (top); Jan Timbrook, 41 (left); Courtesy of Mr. Harry Downie, 42; © Juanita Centeno, 45 (right)

SuperStock International, Inc.–© R. Spencer, 12

© Julie Tumamait–45 (left)

UPI/Bettmann–5

Valan–© Stephen J. Krasemann, 21, 22 (inset)

© Tom Dunnington–Maps 10, 21

COVER: Chumash cave painting

Project Editor: Fran Dyra
Design: Margrit Fiddle

Library of Congress Cataloging-in-Publication Data

Duvall, Jill D.
    The Chumash / by Jill D. Duvall.
        p.   cm.–(A New true book)
    Includes index.
    ISBN 0-516-01052-2
    1.   Chumashan Indians–History–Juvenile literature.
2.   Chumashan Indians–Social life and customs–
Juvenile Literature.   [1.   Chumashan Indians.
2.   Indians of North America.]   I.   Title.
E99.C815L45   1994
979'.004975–dc20   93-36672
                                                       CIP
                                                         AC

TABLE OF CONTENTS

THE CHUMASH

For at least 9,000 years, the place we call California was home to many different tribes of people. One of the oldest and largest of these groups was the Chumash.

Groups of Chumash lived on the mainland as well as on islands in the Pacific Ocean. Sometimes, people living on the mainland referred to the islanders

Juan Justo in 1927.
He was the last person
of 100 percent
Chumash ancestry.

as "those who make shell
bead money," or *Chumash.*
This is now the name
used for all the
California Indian groups
who spoke the same
"Chumash" language.

John P. Harrington (second from left) talking to Chumash
people about their language and culture

LEARNING
ABOUT THE CHUMASH

We have known about
the Chumash people for
a long time.

Early in the 1900s,
a hardworking man,
John P. Harrington,

spent a great deal of time talking with some of the Chumash who had studied their own history. Harrington wrote thousands of pages of notes. They are now in a collection at the Smithsonian Institution in Washington, D.C.

One of the most famous Chumash to talk with Harrington was Fernando Librado. His Chumash name was "Kitsepawit."

Left: In 1912, Kitsepawit built a canoe like
the traditional Chumash redwood canoes.
Right: Kitsepawit

Scholars are working on the
Harrington papers, but it
will take many more years
before we know all that we
can about Kitsepawit's
people. What has been learned
is a fascinating story.

Reenactment of Juan Rodríguez Cabrillo landing in southern California in 1542.

STRANGERS ON SHIPS

Juan Rodríguez Cabrillo was the Portuguese commander of two Spanish ships, *La Victoria* and *San Sebastian*. On the morning of June 27, 1542, he sailed from Navidad,

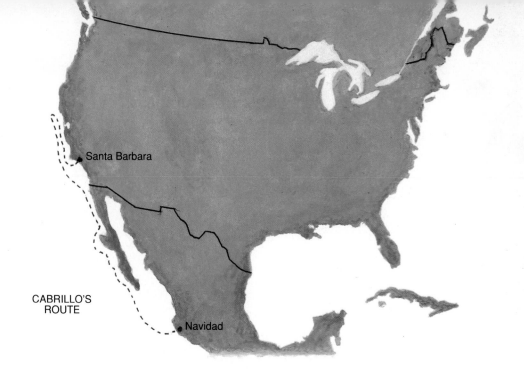

CABRILLO'S
ROUTE

Santa Barbara

Navidad

Mexico, to find a route to China. Mexico was then ruled by Spain. Cabrillo was exploring for Spain.

On October 10, Cabrillo's ships sailed into a beautiful channel. Its name is now Santa Barbara Channel.

What the men saw amazed them. A large number of canoes left the shore and raced to the ships. In each canoe were at least twelve strong men.

Descriptions of this event are filled with praise for the greeting party. They carried gifts of foods, shell beads, animal skins, and other items from their people. During this and later meetings with strangers, the Chumash were very generous and friendly.

The Chumash homeland included the Santa Ynez Mountains near what is now Santa Barbara, California.

On that day in 1542, Juan Cabrillo claimed the area for Spain. The friendly Chumash were unaware of Cabrillo's declaration. It is certain that they would have been unwilling to accept anyone as ruler over them.

A LANGUAGE GROUP

We know the Chumash were not organized into a single group. There was no leader of all the tribes or families. What made them a single group was their type of language. It was called Hokan.

Life must have been very pleasant for the Chumash. Food was

A Chumash mother preparing acorn meal while
her baby rests in a cozy cradle

plentiful and the climate
was usually good. Planting
crops was not necessary.
Whatever they needed was
provided by nature.

These neighboring peoples
were generally peaceful. If

fighting did occur, it was for revenge, not territory. Battles were often fought by ritual. Feathers were tossed into the air by both sides. This meant the contest was to begin. Warriors lined up opposite each other. One at a time, they shot arrows at their opponents until one was injured or killed. Honor was thereby restored to both sides. The fighting was finished.

SYUHTUN

Santa Barbara, as the Spanish called it, was really the village the Chumash called Syuhtun. It was their largest village and had perhaps as many as 1,000 people.

Don Gaspar de Portolá, an explorer, traveled by mule train to Syuhtun in 1769. He saw most of the things that Cabrillo and his men had seen over 200 years before.

Two Franciscan friars

A Chumash village contained many houses,
which were built of wooden poles and matting.

were traveling with Don
Portolá. The diaries of
Juan Crespí and Francisco
Gómez have added greatly
to our knowledge of the
Chumash.

In Syuhtun, or Santa
Barbara, they saw

many houses. They described them very clearly. Houses were built of poles bent over and lashed together at the top. A thick matting called thatch covered the poles. At the center of each

A Chumash house

house was a place for the cooking fire. Smoke rose straight up through a hole in the ceiling. Around the insides of the houses, beds were raised on platforms. Skins and other types of blankets covered the beds. Around each hung mats made of rushes. These made the beds private and cozy. Several families could live in the larger houses.

Houses were arranged in long rows separated by narrow streets. Every village had at least one sweathouse. Today these are called *temescals*. The Chumash sat around a very hot fire and talked. Soon they were perspiring heavily. Then they ran and jumped into ice-cold water.

Santa Cruz Island lies in
Santa Barbara Channel.

Enlarged area

Morro Bay

Santa Cruz Is.

Malibu

San
Miguel
Is.

Santa Inez Is.

Los Angeles

Anacapa Is.

DESIGNERS AND ENGINEERS

Chumash villages were
all along the Pacific Coast
from Malibu to San Luis
Obispo. Smaller settlements
were on ocean islands near
the shore. These islands are
now Santa Cruz, Santa Rosa,
Anacapa, and San Miguel.
Many California towns

Chumash fishermen often paddled their canoes out to the Channel Islands.
Inset: Blooming wildflowers cover a valley on Santa Cruz Island.

have names that are Spanish versions of Chumash words.

The Chumash were excellent fishermen and craftsmen. *Tomol* is the Chumash name for their unique canoe. Only certain men were allowed to make canoes. Using whalebone wedges and deer antlers, they split apart redwood trees that had been uprooted by storms farther north and washed up on their beaches. Sharpened Pismo clam shells and stone knives smoothed the planks. Sharkskin made excellent "sandpaper." The Chumash used tar for sealing their boats.

The *tomols* were engineering wonders.

A soapstone dish full of tar (above). The tar was used for sealing the seams of boats. Twined water bottle (right)

There was no framework inside the canoes. Long planks were joined with plant-fiber string laced through holes. The holes were covered with tar.

A copy of a Chumash *tomol* shown at Santa Barbara in 1976. Native Americans in traditional Chumash dress paddled the canoe.

Center braces made the canoes strong. The oars were very long and the rowers dipped first one end and then the other into the water. The boats were light and fast.

While the Chumash were fishing, they often drifted with the current. At other times, they pulled tops of heavy kelp leaves over the sides of the canoe to keep it steady. These expert fishermen developed hooks, harpoons, sinkers, and spears.

This photo shows the steps used to cut fishhooks from shells.

CHIEFS AND CEREMONIES

Villages always had ceremonial grounds and game areas. It was the duty of the village chief to make sure food and water were available for everyone. The chiefs were usually men, but there were some women who became chiefs after their fathers or older male relatives died.

A male chief often married more than one

woman. No one else was
allowed to have more than
one spouse. The chief
appointed the supervisor
of tribal festivals and
named the messenger of
the tribe. Chumash words
for chief, festival leader,
and messenger are *wot*,
paha, and *ksen*.

The Chumash buried their dead. Every village had a cemetery on its outskirts. Each grave had a painted pole placed in the center. Items that had belonged to the person were placed in the grave to show respect.

The Chumash enjoyed playing many games. Their favorites were hoop-and-pole, shinny (a kind of hockey), and gambling. Dice made from walnut shells and valuable beads cut from

seashells
were used
in gambling
games.
Dancing was
also very
important. The
Chumash
made whistles,
flutes, rattles,
and other
musical
instruments
from bone,
wood, reeds,
and shells.

Chumash gambling game with
walnut-shell dice (above) and
a Chumash painted gourd (below)

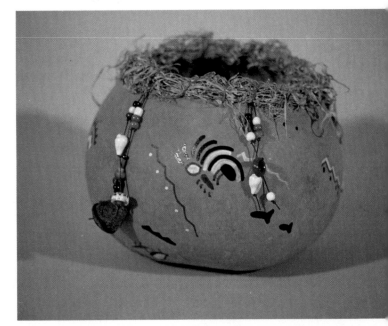

CHUMASH BELIEFS

Chumash beliefs were based upon the things they saw around them. At the Hutash festival, held in the late summer, the Chumash gave thanks for the plants, animals, and especially for a good acorn crop. Hutash honored the Earth Goddess.

At the winter solstice, shamans performed a ritual to bring the sun

back to shine on the
earth. Winter solstice, the
shortest day of the year, is
in our month of December.

These were the two
most important festivals,
but there were many more.
Neighboring people came
to the festivals and brought
many things to trade.
Shell bead money and
barter were both used.

To the Chumash, earth was
the "World of the People."
Two giant serpents held
up the earth, which was

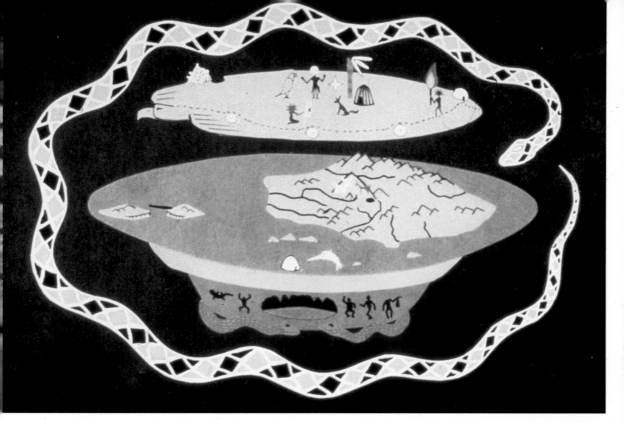

This drawing of Chumash beliefs shows the home of the Sky People, held up by an eagle. Below is the earth—the World of the People.

surrounded by water. According to Chumash stories, earthquakes, volcanoes, and tidal waves were caused by the serpents moving about.

Above the "World of the People" was a huge eagle

Acorns, the seeds of oak trees, were an important food for the Chumash. The seeds were ground into meal, which was boiled like thick soup or mush.

whose wings held up the sky. It was there the Sky People lived. When they became angry, thunder, lightning, and fierce storms came down upon the Chumash.

Another belief of the Chumash was that the "First People" had been transformed

into the plants and animals
of their own world. These
were the ancient people who
at first had been much like
themselves.

A great flood caused all
the "First People" to die.
When they returned to earth,
just before the Chumash came,
great powers had been given
to them. When they wished,
they could become plants
or animals. Just as
quickly, they could shift
back again.

Kitsepawit and other

Vincent Tumamait,
a Chumash elder,
at the Chumash
Today program in
Santa Barbara
in 1989

Chumash learned the wonderful
stories about Coyote, Lizard,
Bat, Roadrunner, Falcon,
Toad, and Woodpecker.
They told the stories over
and over.

STUDYING THEIR WORLD

Many of the Chumash were students of astronomy, medicine, nature, and people. There were special shamans who knew which plant medicines and which treatments to use for

Rafael Solares, a Chumash shaman, photographed in 1878.

illnesses. When Chumash
tribal life was still
strong, everyone believed
in the power of these
things.

Animals also had great
powers. These powers
could be shared by people.
Through dreams, each
person found out what his
or her animal power was.
A likeness of this animal
was made from wood,
stone, or bone. It was
carried by the person
until death.

WORDS AND PICTURES

Words were considered the most powerful things in the "World of the People." Writing words would make them lose their power. Even though we have not been able to read the words of these

The mysterious Chumash paintings do not seem to tell stories. The artists were not trying to show real animals.

interesting people, we do know some of the things they imagined.

Fantastic pictures, called pictographs, were painted deep in caves, on mountain walls, and on flat rocks exposed to the weather. Strange and fascinating creatures are in these paintings, which are found throughout Chumash territory.

Father Junípero Serra (above) was a Franciscan missionary in America. In 1772, he founded the Mission Santa Barbara (left) in the Chumash territory.

CHANGE AND THE END

The Chumash life began to disappear in the 1770s. Father Junípero Serra, a Franciscan priest, began setting up Catholic missions in Chumash territory.

To Father Serra, the Native Americans were in need of religion and

41

A photo taken in 1882 shows some of the last Native Americans to live at a California mission.

training for "useful" work. Unfortunately, his ideas were from an entirely different world, the world of Europe. He did not understand the Chumash culture.

The Indians were encouraged to wear too much clothing for their climate and lifestyle. They began eating strange foods and were made

to work too hard at jobs
they disliked. Village life
was eventually broken
apart. Gradually, Indians
began living at the missions.
Their understanding of
nature was replaced by
Christianity. Their language
was replaced by Spanish.

In 1824, Mexico declared
itself free of Spanish
rule, and soon the 21
missions in California
were taken away from the
Catholic Church. The land
was supposed to be

given to the mission
Indians. It was thought
they could become farmers
and ranchers.

The plan did not work.
Farming had never been part
of the Chumash style of life.
Most of the land went to
Spanish and Mexican settlers.
The Chumash could not go
back to their old way of life.

After gold was discovered
in northern California,
many more people moved
there. In 1850, California
became one of the

Chumash descendants still live in southern California. They are working to keep their history and traditions alive.

United States of America.

Today, about 3,000 people can trace their family history to a Chumash ancestor. Many of them are working with scholars so that these peaceful, artistic people will never be forgotten.

WORDS YOU SHOULD KNOW

acorn (A • korn)–the nutlike seed of an oak tree

ancient (AIN • shint)–very old; living long ago

astronomy (ah • STRAH • nuh • mee)–the study of the moon and stars and other objects in the sky

ceremonial (sair • ih • MOAN • ee • al)–used for religious celebrations

channel (CHAN • il)–a narrow body of water between two landmasses

current (KER • int)–a flow of ocean water in a certain direction, like a river in the sea

diary (DYE • uh • ree)–a written record of the daily happenings in a person's life

fascinating (FASS • in • nay • ting)–having great interest; appealing

friar (FRY • er)–a member of a religious community

harpoon (har • POON)–a long stick with a hooked, pointed end, thrown by fishermen to spear fish

pictograph (PIK • tuh • graf)–a painting on rocks

redwood (RED • wood)–a huge evergreen tree that grows in California

ritual (RIT • choo • il)–a special set of actions used in religious ceremonies

rushes (RUSH • iz)–plants with long, stiff stems that grow in water

shaman (SHAH • min)–a person who could cure diseases

sinew (SIN • yoo)–strong, white cord that attaches muscles to bones

sinker (SING • ker)–a heavy weight, such as a piece of lead, used to hold fish bait low in the water

solstice (SOLE • stiss)–the time of year when the sun reaches the point farthest north or south of the equator

tribe (TRYBE)–a group of people related by blood and customs

INDEX

About the Author

Jill D. Duvall is a political scientist who received an M.A. from Georgetown University in 1976. Since then, her research and writing have included a variety of national and international issues. Among these are world hunger, alternative energy, human rights, cross-cultural and interracial relationships. One of her current endeavors is a study of ancient goddess cultures. Ms. Duvall proudly serves as a member of the Board of Managers of the Glenn Mills Schools, a facility that is revolutionizing methods for rehabilitating male juvenile delinquents.